EUPHONICS FOR WRITERS

by Rayne Hall

EUPHONICS FOR WRITERS

Copyright Rayne Hall © 2015 (text and images)
(March 2016 Edition)
Cover art and design by Erica Syverson
Interior illustrations by Hanna-Riikka

All rights reserved. Do not reproduce the content in whole or in part without the author's written permission.

CONTENTS

INTRODUCTION 5
PART 1: THE SOUND EFFECT THESAURUS 7
'B' FOR BOLDNESS, BRUTALITY AND BULLYING 9
'B' FOR HUMOUR, ROUND OBJECTS AND BIG PEOPLE 11
'CH' AND 'J' FOR CHEER AND JOY 13
'D' FOR SQUALOR, DEFEAT AND DESPAIR 15
'EE' FOR CREEPINESS AND FEAR 17
'F' FOR SUPERFICIAL FLOURISHES AND FRIVOLOUS FUN 19
'G' FOR GRUNGE, GRIT, BOGS AND OOZING SLIME 21
'H' FOR HIGH PLACES, LOFTY ASPIRATIONS, SUFFERING
AND HAUGHTY ATTITUDES 23
'I' FOR ITSY-BITSY LITTLE THINGS 26
'L' FOR SENSUALITY, IDLENESS AND LEISURE 28
'K' FOR CUTS, CLAWS AND ATTACKS 30
'M' FOR MOTHER, MELANCHOLY, HOME AND COMFORTS 32
'N' FOR BANS, CONTEMPT AND REFUSALS 34
'O/OH' FOR HONOURABLE INTENTIONS, BRAVE
SUFFERING AND NOBLE HEROES 36
'OO' AND 'OW' FOR SPOOKS, FOREBODING,
GLOOM AND DOOM 38
'P' FOR MASCULINITY, POWER AND PRIDE 40
'R' FOR HURRY AND SPEED 43
'S' FOR SPOOKY EXPERIENCES AND WHISPERED SECRETS 45
FOR SLIMY STUFF, SLIPSHOD WORK, UNDERHAND
METHODS, LOWER CLASSES AND SLIPPERY SITUATIONS 47

'SN' FOR SECRET MOVEMENTS, CONTEMPT,
TREACHERY AND SNEAK ATTACKS 49

'STR' FOR STRICT RULES, DISCIPLINE AND RESTRICTIONS 51

'TR' AND 'T+R' FOR TRICKERY, BREWING TROUBLE
AND TERRIBLE WEATHER 53

'W' OVERWHELMING FORCES, WILD WEATHER
AND ANYTHING WET 55

'Z' FOR DIZZINESS, CONFUSION AND TOO MUCH DRINK 57

PART 2: SOUND PLACEMENT AND RHYTHM 59

SPECIAL SPICE: ALLITERATION 60

DISCREET INSIDER JOBS: ASSONANCE AND CONSONANCE 62

WHEN THE SOUND IS THE WORD: ONOMATOPOEIA 63

KEEP THE BEST FOR LAST: BACKLOADING 64

SENTENCE LENGTH: VARIETY AND PURPOSE 66

SENTENCE STRUCTURE 68

REPEAT, REPEAT, REPEAT... BUT SPARINGLY,
VERY SPARINGLY 71

HURRY OR TEDIUM? MAKE LISTS 75

TEST YOUR EUPHONICS SKILLS 78

SAMPLE STORY: TAKE ME TO ST. ROCH'S 80

SAMPLE STORY: THE COLOUR OF DISHONOUR 89

DEAR READER 104

ACKNOWLEDGEMENTS 105

SAMPLE: WRITING VIVID SETTINGS *(Writer's Craft Book 10)* 106

INTRODUCTION

Learn how to touch your readers' subconscious with subtle tricks.

Certain sounds have certain effects on the psyche. By using words which include those sounds, you influence how the reader feels.

Euphonic techniques are popular in poetry, but seldom used in prose. This guide shows how you can apply them to make your prose fiction sparkle.

For the purpose of this book, I define euphonics as 'the use of sound devices for prose writing'. Poets, musicians and special effects engineers have their own definitions.

I'll show you which sounds to apply in order to manipulate your readers' psyche the way you want. You'll learn how to impress your readers with power, how to make their hearts race with urgency, how to creep them out and how to let them linger in a sensual scene.

Part 1 is a thesaurus of sound effects where you can look up the best sounds to enhance the mood of your scene.

In Part 2, you'll learn how and when to apply the sounds and how to combine them with rhythm for best effect.

This book isn't meant as a definitive scholarly tome for academics, but a practical kit for working authors who want to refine their voice. I'll avoid literary theory and grammatical jargon. Instead, I'll give you useful tools.

Novice writers can have inspiring fun playing with euphonics. In the hands of skilled writers—for whom this guide is intended—euphonics are power tools.

Euphonics can't replace basic fiction crafting skills, but they can add impact and polish to a well-written piece.

In print, the effects are very subtle, serving only to enhance what's already there, and need to be combined with other techniques. But

Euphonics for Writers

if you plan to perform author readings or release an audiobook, the euphonics will hold listeners enthralled with poetic power.

I'm writing in British English. Some spellings, grammatical rules and word choices differ from American English, but the euphonic effects are the same.

Now open your manuscript draft and give it that special polish.

Rayne

PART 1:
THE SOUND EFFECT THESAURUS

Here you'll find sounds to create certain moods in the reader's mind: 'EE' gives a creepy sensation, while 'R' creates a sense of hurry and speed, and 'P' hints at masculinity, authority and pride.

I suggest you read through the thesaurus once to discover what's there and get a feel for possibilities. Then you choose the scene you want to revise, and pick the sound—or sounds—to bring about the desired mood.

In each section, Cartoon Kitty will show what the effects mean to a cat.

Collect suitable words and either list them on your computer, or write them on slips of paper (coloured card is nice), and put them in a pretty basket to pick out and play with. Use them to replace some words in your manuscript.

But please don't get carried away using unsuitable words for the sake of euphonics. Content is always more important than sound.

English is a strongly euphonic language, and many words contain sounds which suit their content. Words like *creak, eerie, secret,* and *screech*, for example, create a creepy feel. Each thesaurus section lists such words, as well as others which don't carry that meaning but hold the same sound and can serve to enrich the effect.

For those of you who like technical terms, the effect of sound creating word meaning is called 'phonosemantics'.

Euphonic sounds will amplify the effects of your skilfully crafted writing, but they can't create what isn't there. I can't emphasise this enough. On their own, the sounds won't work.

Apply the sounds with a light brush, like subtle make-up. The reader should not be aware of the technique, only of the resulting beauty.

'B' FOR BOLDNESS, BRUTALITY AND BULLYING

The letter 'B', especially at the beginning of words, creates an impression of unpleasantly assertive, aggressive behaviour. Many words in the English language convey these meanings.

They describe aggressive people: *bully, bastard, bitch, rabble, bouncer,* assertiveness especially of the grating kind: *bold, big, broad, brazen, blatant, bossy, brag, boast, bluster,* violent actions and attitudes: *beat, belt, bash, bang, blow, box, brawl, grab, jab, stab, bad, clobber, blast, rob, brutal, bust, bump, bruise.*

Besides those words, you can use others which don't carry this meaning but bolster the effect by repeating the 'B' sound: *oboe, blue, black, brown, bag, ball, bull, bear, but, bitter, pulse, band, bicker, oblige, abide, abode, buddy, bin, bridge, bell, bed, better, beggar, begin, boil, gable, stable, job, able, marble, basil, broadcast, bird, breeches, boomerang, bulldog, bleet, blood, abode, boat.* These are just a starting point for you—you can use any words you like.

Usage examples: your fictional bully may drink beer rather than wine, and boil his beef rather than stew his mutton.

When To Use 'B' Sounds

- to create an atmosphere of violence
- for physical fights
- to show bullying
- to characterise a person who enjoys intimidating others

Caution: the 'B' sound also increases comedic effects. More about that in the next section.

'B' FOR HUMOUR, ROUND OBJECTS AND BIG PEOPLE

In the previous section, we looked at how the 'B' sound can evoke a sense of bullying and brutality. Here we'll look at a different effect—humour. A stand-up comedian and author, V.G. Lee, taught me this trick: use words with 'B' and the audience will laugh more at your jokes.

Many English words with 'B' suggest a comedic element: *bumble, stumble, bungle, slob, brag, jumble, fumble, embarrass, imbibe, blush, shambles, slobber, gobble, blob, burlesque, gambol, buffoon.*

Euphonics for Writers

'B' also hints at round shapes, large objects and overweight bodies: *ball, globe, barrel, tub, knob, basket, baggy, billow, bubble, bowl, breast, bosom, bust, butt, belly, big, abs, flabby, obese.*

To increase the effect, use words of unrelated meanings which contain the 'B' sound: *badger, rub, snub, stub, bicker, drab, habit, body, broom, hob, gob, robe, ramble, amble, bone, begin, rubber, boat, bald, boil, baby, barge, bundle, brown, blue, bow, browse, object.* Also see the suggestions in the previous section.

Usage examples: the drinkers sit between the beer barrels rather than among the casks of ale. A plump woman may be big-bosomed rather than large-chested. Instead of devouring the steamed cauliflower, the characters gobble up the boiled broccoli.

When To Use 'B' Sounds

- in funny scenes
- when writing slapstick and comedy
- to show a drunken or clumsy person's movements
- to hint at a character's obesity without spelling it out
- to emphasise the plumpness or roundness of objects
- for scenes of brutal violence (see previous section)

At this stage you may wonder how to keep the two 'B' effects apart, and if by shooting for one you may accidentally hit the other. Don't worry. The euphonics are so subtle, they won't create a meaning of their own. Rather, they strengthen what's already there. So if you've written a violent fight scene, adding 'B' sounds will emphasise the brutality, and in a slapstick comedy, 'B' will increase the humour.

However, euphonics need to be applied with a light brush. If you use too many 'B' sounds too close together, the effect will be comedic whether you intend it or not.

'CH' AND 'J' FOR CHEER AND JOY

The similar sounds 'J' and CH' express a jubilant mood, celebrating achievement: j*oy, cheer, jubilation, jamboree, jolly, jaunt, chuckle, cherish, chirp, achieve, jester, enjoy.*

Here's a collection of words which are thematically unrelated, but can enhance the effect if they suit your story: *touch, cheap, exchange, charm, juggle, jiggle, joint, jug, jar, pitcher, chequered, catch, chin.*

Usage examples: at the victory feast, the characters may enjoy a joint of beef, a jug of ale and a juggling display, rather than a rib of beef, a bottle of beer and a dance show. They may celebrate the jubilee in January rather than the anniversary in November.

When To Use 'CH' and 'J' Sounds

- when characters are relieved and happy, especially after a tense situation or an ordeal
- for merry celebrations
- for scenes of triumph

Tip: for official celebrations, such as national holidays and triumphal processions, use the 'P' sound as well as the 'CH/J'. For frivolous fun, blend the 'CH/J' with 'F', and for laid-back partying, combine 'CH/J' with 'L'.

'D' FOR SQUALOR, DEFEAT AND DESPAIR

The 'D' sound creates a dejected mood: *down, dump, dejected, dead, damp, defeated, deflated, drag, dull, ditch, bad, shroud, cloud, drugged, drunk, drab, dreich* (a Scots word for abysmal wet grey weather).

Other—thematically unconnected—words you can use to repeat the 'D' sound in your scenes: *dog, dart, mad, head, dill, dagger, desk, lad, spade, made, den, disk, mood, hood, rod, loud, mound, hand, land, sand, dip, dry.*

Euphonics for Writers

When To Use 'D' Sounds

- when your main character has lost all hope
- unhappiness
- to convey a depressed mood without spending many paragraphs describing it
- after a fight or battle ending in defeat
- when an important or well-liked character has died

Usage examples: after the fight is lost, the surviving loser may not limp off the battlefield past corpses and collapse in a wet trench, but drag himself past dead bodies until he collapses in a damp ditch.

'EE' FOR CREEPINESS AND FEAR

The 'EE' sound creates a creepy effect in the reader's mind. Many words in the English language describe spooky, eerie, frightening effects and contain this sound: *creak, fear, sheer, squeak, seelie, secret, flee, squeal, conceal, fear, creep, steep, weep, deep, shriek, scream.*

Here are some other words you can use to add to the effect: *clear, steal, ear, dear, wheel, meal, leap, cheap, heap, keep, reap, sheep, cleave, sheaf, leaf, leave, siege, sieve, sleeve, dream, beam, reeve, heave, see, seal, reprieve.*

When To Use 'EE' Sounds

- for ghost stories
- for horror fiction
- for creepy locations
- for describing eerie sights and sounds
- when the Point-of-View character is frightened
- whenever you want to scare your readers

Usage examples: your heroine drinks tea rather than hot chocolate in the castle's keep, and on the steep slopes graze sheep, not cows.

Tip: To increase the spookiness, combine words with 'EE' and 'S' sounds.

'F' FOR SUPERFICIAL FLOURISHES AND FRIVOLOUS FUN

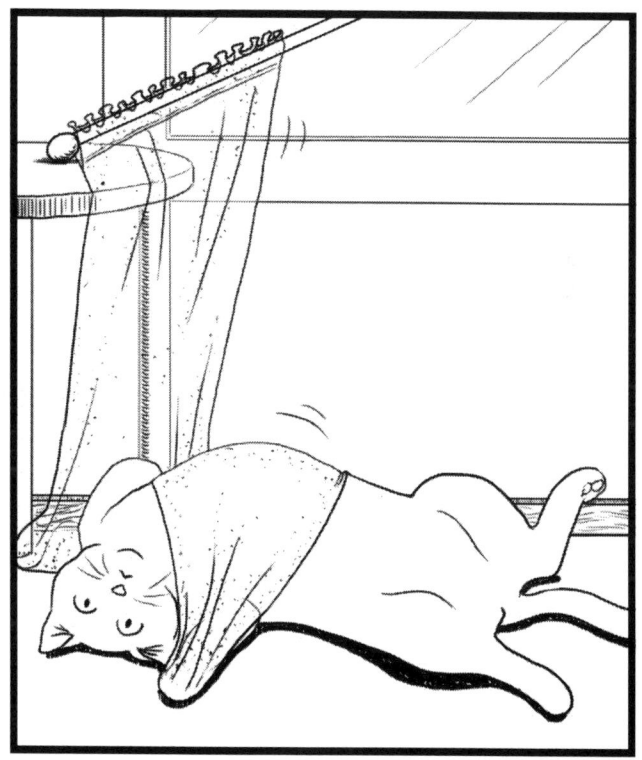

The 'F' sound is playful, carefree, unconcerned with serious matters. It suits superficial characters and fun activities: *flighty, flapper, folly, foolish, flutter, fake, carefree, fête, festive, feast, flirt, fast, fantasy, butterfly, free, affable, flamboyant, flit, fabulous, flippant, frolic, fun, frivolous, fling, flash, flush, fair, fop, flibbertigibbet.*

It's also great for adornment: *ruffles, frippery, flourishes, flair, frills, fringe, fashion, frock, feather, flowery, filigree.*

Other words with unrelated meanings but the same sound effect: *flock, finger, flag, flank, fill, flow, food, fanfare, filly, fellow, finger, fist, fork, fig, follow, film, fright, effort, fish, flask, fever, few, far, fame, fester, ferry, fart.*

When To Use 'F' Sounds

- to describe light entertainment such as parties and funfairs
- for superficial, flamboyant, foppish characters
- to describe the clothes of a fashionista
- when a character acts foolishly without thought of the consequences
- to show a carefree situation before tragedy strikes

Usage examples: the character may wear a flowery frock rather than a printed dress when she attends the village fair, and she might even flutter her fan to seek a flirtation. At the church fête, you can find fast food stalls, a raffle, lots of flags and perhaps a children's fancy dress competition. The thief filches a flask rather than steals a bottle.

Tip: the 'F' sound combines well with 'L' to create a sense of careless, idle pleasures or to show a character who is lazy as well as superficial.

'G' FOR GRUNGE, GRIT, BOGS AND OOZING SLIME

The 'G' sound adds a layer of unpleasantness and disgust: *greasy, gloom, grime, glum, gloom, gall, guts, greed, garbage, grievous, grunge, grisly, gritty, glutinous,* often in the context of slime and goo: *gurgle, glob, bog, gummy, gooey, soggy, clogged.*

Unrelated words with the same sound can add to the effect. Here are some suggestions: *grope, grab, grip, great, garage, garland, hog, pig, gift, gone, gallant, get, garden, guilt, gulp.*

Usage examples: there's a gurgle in the kitchen sink's downpipe, green goo oozes from the plughole... and a tentacle wriggles out.

The prisoner gropes her way through the dark, touching soggy straw and a greasy pillow.

When To Use the 'G' sound

- to create a sense of gritty realism
- when you want to arouse a sense of disgust in the reader
- for Lovecraftian fiction with lots of slime
- to show unacceptable living conditions, e.g. in a slum or a dungeon

Tip: to show true squalor, combine several 'G' and 'D' words in the same paragraph. For Lovecraftian slime-oozing monsters, mix 'G' with 'SL'.

'H' FOR HIGH PLACES, LOFTY ASPIRATIONS, SUFFERING AND HAUGHTY ATTITUDES

The sound 'H' hints at something high up—places, objects, people, either physically or metaphorically: *heaven, hilltop, hierophant, hierarchy, head.* It may signify lofty aspirations: *hope, hankering,* and virtuous attitudes:*(helpfulness, honour, happiness, honesty, humility, heart.*

Another effect is to convey a person's arrogance: *haughty, high and mighty, on a high horse, hubris.*

Euphonics for Writers

Finally, it may indicate suffering: *hell, heat, harassment, hardship, horror, hearse, hassle, haggard, helpless, haunted, horrible, harm, hatred, hurt.*

Other words with the 'H' sound can add to the desired effect: *hunt, hatch, hollow, hint, hinder, hark, hear, house, home, humid, haste, hearsay, hobble, hand, hound.*

Usage examples: instead of listening to divine music, the character hears heavenly tunes. Instead of wishing to go back, he hopes to go home.

In the English language, the pronounced 'H' sound comes almost always at the beginning of the word (alliteration—see Part 2 of this guide). When the 'H' appears elsewhere, it's part of a different sound: *ache, flesh, other.* Those related sounds can create the same effect, but in much diluted strength.

Words beginning with 'H' are often paired: *high hopes, heaven and hell, head and heart, high horse, helping hand, hot as hell, heavenly host.* Careful: although these paired words intensify the euphonic effect, they are so common ('clichés') that they can make your writing sound hackneyed.

When To Use the 'H' Sound:

- when writing about a character's ambitions, especially if those are either idealistic or castles in the air
- to describe something out of the Point-of-View character's reach
- for characters who are high up in the pecking order, to remind others of this
- for arrogant characters

Tip: if you've mastered the use of euphonics, consider combining the 'H' with other sounds. 'H' plus 'O' is perfect for noble aspirations. 'H' plus 'L' conveys idle daydreams not backed by action,

'H' plus 'SL' can amplify racial or class arrogance, 'H' plus 'B' amplifies brutality against helpless victims, and 'H' plus 'D' serves to emphasise social injustice.

'I' FOR ITSY-BITSY LITTLE THINGS

The short 'I' sound indicates something small: *wisp, bikini, hint, whiff, little, belittle, thin, skinny, itsy-bitsy, mini, kitten, nit, hint, nip, blip, bit, sweet, chip, sip, glitch, whimper, trivial,* and is common in words for small or young people: *kid, children, nipper, slip, miss, stripling, whippersnapper, imp, pixie, chit.*

It also conveys rapid movements: *flick, flip, hit, whisk, snip, rip, swift.*

Other words you can use: *wit, fit, tin, win, silly, list, wind, mist, rid, silly, silt, sit, sift, lift, shift, mid, slick, pin, sick, listen, glisten, livid, rigid, ilk, gift, switch, itch, fling.*

Usage examples: when the gang leader addresses his followers, he plays down the strength of his enemies by describing them as skinny kids. The Regency lady talks of her love rival as a silly chit, and the engineer responsible for the technical failure calls it a simple glitch.

When To Use the Short 'I' Sound

- to emphasise how tiny something is
- to create a contrast with something or someone much taller
- in dialogue when a character belittles someone else or trivialises a situation

'L' FOR SENSUALITY, IDLENESS AND LEISURE

The 'L' sound conveys idleness and slow relaxation: *slow, idle, lazy, leisure, mellow, lie, linger, loll, relax, pleasant, pillow, laid-back.*

It also evokes erotic pleasures and desires: *sensuality, lick, lap, tickle, leer, lecherous, lips, labia, lesbian, lust, lascivious.*

It may also suggest a passive, unresisting nature: *pliant, flexible, yielding, comply.*

Other words which don't have a specific meaning of laziness or sensuality but can evoke that mood through their sound include: *laugh, chuckle, long, languish, language, lurid, pale, shell, wall, pile, plunder, pill, melon, light, lad, loud, delay, last.*

Usage example: your idler may linger on yellow pillows instead of red cushions, and lick his lips after sampling melon slices and lobster rather than orange quarters and carp.

When To Use 'L' Sounds

- to show lazy characters doing nothing when they should be working
- for those brief moments when your hero enjoys peaceful relaxation between ordeals
- for erotic fiction, especially leisurely, drawn-out, sensuous experiences
- to create erotic tension in other genres, especially if you want to convey the character's desires without spelling them out graphically
- when a character chooses to give in rather than to resist

Tip: skilled writers can create subtle yet powerful effects by blending 'L' and 'P' sounds in one paragraph, mixing the pliant leisurely sensuality of the 'L' with the rigid, demanding nature of the 'P', or contrasting the laid-back lazy idler with the weapon-carrying authority enforcer. Surprisingly often, the English language even combines the two sounds in a single word, for instance, *pliable, plead, supply, pillow, plunder, lap, leap, grapple, pole, lip, pill, plight.*

'K' FOR CUTS, CLAWS AND ATTACKS

The 'K' sound—which may be spelled 'c', 'q' or 'ck'—represents hard, sharp, painful events, whether these are physical actions or verbal attacks.

This makes the sound great for fight scenes: *hook, block, duck, attack, cull, squash, crush, break, fracture, kill,* and verbal altercations: *sarcastic, quote, squabble, remark, quarrel, squirm, criticism, caustic, quibble.* Many 'K' words represent sharp blades and what they do: *sickle, hack, secateurs, cut, claw, castrate, scalp, scar.*

Sometimes, the 'K' in those words isn't actually heard, although it is written: *knife, knuckle, knock.*

Thematically unrelated words you can use to reinforce the 'K' effect in your scene: *key, cat, car, create, core, rack, black, squat, career, concentrate, correct, square, cart, carriage, king, queer, clasp, crutch, catch, deflect, duct, shock, clock, click, rock.*

Usage example: under attack, the character doesn't hide behind the trailer, but ducks behind the cart. Instead of gripping the knife, he clutches it.

When To Use 'K' sounds

- for physical fights, especially with swords or knives
- for torture scenes
- for verbal arguments
- to represent sharp-bladed items
- to convey sharp, painful situations

Tip: experienced writers can combine the 'K' sound with 'R' words to create the fast pace of a knife fight, or with 'B' to convey the brutal reality of fighting.

'M' FOR MOTHER, MELANCHOLY, HOME AND COMFORTS

The 'M' sound is warm, gentle, homely, welcoming: *comfort, mild, merciful, mollycoddling, mulled, mellow, warmth, amiable, embrace, home, comfort, ambience, meal,* as well as motherly: *mother, mum, mammal, maternal, madonna, moon, mare, womb.*

Sometimes, the 'M' sound contributes to a sense of sadness: *morose, misery, mouldy, mourn, melancholy, moody, doom, glum.*

Other words you can use to add to the effect, although their meaning is unrelated: *mean, mush, meek, humble, arm, harm, market, mirth, merry, mask, mantle, mill, mouse, amble, ample, amber.*

Usage examples: the character looks forward to a warm meal at home, rather than a hot supper in his house. He sits in the armchair with a mug of mulled wine, rather than on the couch with a cup of hot spiced wine.

When To Use 'M' Sounds

- for cosy scenes
- happy family scenes
- when the hero returns home after a gruelling adventure
- longing for home and loved ones
- to describe a maternal, strong but gentle character.
- when the Point-of-View character feels melancholy (but not desperate)

Tip: to suggest loving but firm parenting, combine the 'M' with the 'P' sound. The same combination can suggest a powerful benevolent ruler. 'M' combined with 'L' suggests cosy leisure. You can also add 'M' to 'D' to let the reader share a character's depression.

'N' FOR BANS, CONTEMPT AND REFUSALS

The 'N' sound signals 'no!' It suggests that something is forbidden: *no, nothing, never, nix, non, banned, denial, negative, nope, nothing, nowhere, nobody, sin, decline, deny.* The negative connotations of this sound are also contained in the prefix 'un-': *unacceptable, undesirable, ungodly, unreasonable, uncouth.*

Remarkably, the word 'no' in many languages starts with the 'N' sound: *nein, non, nay, ne, nee, net, niama, neniu, ningunha, nem, næ, nahīṁ.*

In addition, 'N' can also signify a contemptuous attitude: *sneer, denigrate, down, contempt, neglect, nit-picking, snub, snobbery.*

Other words you can add to increase the effect: *banner, bannock, banter, answer, night, band, stand, hand, land, mean, stone, want, nerd, need, nasty, naked, noon, grant, town, net, notch, nap.*

Usage examples: citizens may no longer leave the town at night, the grant application is denied, and she sneers down at him.

When To Use 'N' Sounds

- when a request is denied
- when a law or rule forbids the characters to do what they want
- to signify contempt

Tip: the 'N' combines well with 'P' to emphasise the unbending rules of bureaucracy, or with 'H' to show a haughty character's snobbery.

'O/OH' FOR HONOURABLE INTENTIONS, BRAVE SUFFERING AND NOBLE HEROES

The pronunciation of many words in this section varies from country to country, and in many cases it changed over the centuries, so aim for an approximate 'O' or 'OH' rather than an exact sound.

'O/OH' evokes loyalty, nobility and heroism: *honour, glory, noble, hero, throne, god, soul, lord, oath, rouse, follow.* It can also hint at bravely endured adversities: *blow, foe, woes, broken, dole, moan, groan, oppose, cope.*

Other words you can use to repeat the 'O/OH' sound in your paragraphs include: *slow, low, know, mow, show, own, nose, moan, open, close, mote, broke, vote, cloak, coat, moat, throat, globe, globe, whole, oboe, snow, owl, bowl, sole, role.*

Usage examples: if there's music when the beloved heir to the throne dies, a lone oboe playing a slow melody works better than if a saxophone band plays the same tune. The hero may march through the snow-laden storm to meet his foe, rather than through the wet wind to face his enemy. He wears a coat or a cloak, rather than a jacket or a cape.

When To Use 'O/OH' Sounds

- when writing about a noble, heroic character
- when showing a noble, heroic deed
- in speeches intended to arouse loyal or patriotic emotions
- when the noble fight is lost
- when a hero has died for his noble cause

Tips: the 'O/OH' effect combines well with the 'P' sound when writing about a heroic leader or masculine warrior, and with 'N' when the hero denies himself his own needs to serve the greater good. To describe the situation when the noble cause is lost, consider combining 'O/OH' with 'D' to arouse the reader's emotions.

'OO' AND 'OW' FOR SPOOKS, FOREBODING, GLOOM AND DOOM

The 'OO' and 'OW' sounds can create a dark or spooky atmosphere: *gloom, moon, moor, ooze, spook, hoot, mood, moot, soot, owl, howl, clouds, shroud, wound, ooze, growl.*

They can also serve to hint at forthcoming doom and danger: *doom, soothsayer, loom*

Other words to add to your prose to increase the effect: *round, bound, bloom, mound, proud, bout, found, pout, loud, snout, sound, how, cow, cowl, now, found, tool, school, food, root, loot, zoo, pure, cure, hood, room, cool.*

Usage examples: clouds waft past the moon, and an owl hoots. On the mound behind the school house, dark red roses bloom.

When To Use 'OO' and 'OW' Sounds

- for ghost stories and spooky scenes
- to convey a character's sense of foreboding
- to hint at dark events to come of which the characters are not yet aware

Tip: you can combine 'OO' and 'OW' with the very similar 'O' and 'OH' sounds to signify that a noble cause is doomed. To ramp up the spooky effect, mix 'OO' and 'OW' with 'EE' and 'S', and the scene will ooze creepiness.

'P' FOR MASCULINITY, POWER AND PRIDE

The sound of the letter 'P' is masculine, authoritative and proud, and you can use it to evoke a sense of maleness and power.

In the English language, many words containing the letter 'P' convey exactly this meaning.

'P' words are used to express authority: *power, principle, politics, parliament, empire, approve, impose,* a person who wields authority: *president, prelate, prefect, emperor, empress, pastor, priest, prince, pontiff, patriarch.*

Displays of authority and of personal pride also often have a 'P' sound: *parade, palace, portal, pose, display, pomp, peacock, prance, preen, pretend, imposter, importance, impress.*

Words relating to judgement, military, law enforcement and punishment often have the letter 'P': *police, penalty, punishment, appraisal, probe, oppose, probate, approve, passport, apprehend, appeal, troop, platoon, deploy, poll, parish, population, protocol, parochial, position, plead, process, prison.*

Many long stick-like objects contain the letter P: *pole, pile, peg, pillar, pilaster, peak, pike, spear,* and so do the actions carried out with them: *poke, pierce, prong, push, pin, prick, penetrate, point.* Perhaps it's no coincidence that words for the male sexual organ are often 'P' words, too: *penis, prick*, as are many words conveying maleness: *patriarchy, paternal, progenitor.*

Other words you can use to add to the 'P' effect in your paragraphs: *apply, park, perk, pug, puppy, posy, plug, apple, pear, grape apricot, peach, painting, portrait, picture, people, ping, peg, gape, lip, ship, pen, pulse, parchment, palaver, ploy, ape, sap, tap, sip, tip, pillow, pirouette, pry, pray, staple, pry, ploy, slip, plant, peek, peer, nape, plate, platinum, planet, ship, rip, spin, wasp, lamp, ample, shape.*

Usage examples: the warriors don't eat oranges and strawberries, but pears and plums. Outside the emperor's palace, instead of foxgloves flowering among birches, show poppies blooming amidst poplars. The entrance to the court of law doesn't have columns on either side of the door, but pillars flanking the portal.

When To Use 'P' Sounds

- to show unbending authority, bureaucracy or the law
- for a male-only environment such as a boot camp for warriors
- to portray a character who prides himself on his masculinity
- for erotic scenes with male action

- for a display of power, especially if it's pompous
- to portray a proud or pompous character
- for a firm patriarchal society or male-dominated family

Tip: to portray a pompous haughty character, combine the 'P' and 'H' sounds in the same paragraph. For unbending prohibitions, use 'P' with 'N'. For a benevolent ruler, blend 'P' and 'M'.

'R' FOR HURRY AND SPEED

In fast-paced scenes when things happen quickly, words containing the 'R' sound emphasise the speed: *hurry, rush, race, run, rapid, scurry, rip, flurry.*

Here are some more words you can add to the mix: *thrust, ring, roll, red, rage, riot, pare, pour, pore, sore, sour, sure, sire, bray, ray, risk, rebel, round, rust, retch, rasp, rut, car, carriage, cry, arc, arch, rant.*

Usage example: the heroine doesn't pull herself from the villain's clasp and dash across the alley, but she tears herself from his grip and races across the road.

When To Use 'R' Sounds

- whenever you want to achieve a fast pace in your writing
- when a character is in a great hurry and moving fast
- for fight scenes
- for chases and escapes

Tip: in fight scenes the sounds 'R' and 'K' combine well, especially when the combatants fight with swords, knives or daggers. The English language has many words which blend both sounds, perfect for this use: *crack, rack, rock, rookie, rake, strike, stroke, crutch, crotch, cur, curb, curt, court, torque, crop, cry, trick, trap.*

'S' FOR SPOOKY EXPERIENCES AND WHISPERED SECRETS

Words with the 'S' sound, especially when clustered together, create a secretive effect: *discreet, suspicious, confession, mystery, secret*, often of something done quietly or said in low volume: *silent, noiseless, whisper, hiss, lisp*. It also serves to hint at supernatural and spooky presences: *ghost, spectre, presence, spirit, spook*.

Here are some thematically unrelated words which you can add to the mix to increase the effect: *spin, supper, sin, spine, sound, sing, sow, sew, sad, send, haste, waste, rest, jest, chest, clasp, rasp, wasp, stain, stun, start, stag, staff, stuff, sting, star, stare, stilt, sill, silt, stoop, sinister, glisten, sister, sibling.*

Usage examples: the character may whisper secrets to his sibling, rather than confide them to his brother.

When To Use 'S' Sounds

- for ghost stories
- for supernatural happenings (or suspicions of supernatural events)
- when characters don't wish to be noticed or overheard
- for whispered secrets

Tip: if you're creating a ghost story or a creepy paranormal scene, the 'S' sound combined with 'EE' will send shudders down the reader's spine. For this, you can simply mix 'S' words and 'EE' words, but the English language is also rich in words containing both sounds, such as *seep, sleep, secret, see, steep, sweet, keys, sneeze, scream, squeal, screech.*

You may have noticed that quite a few euphonic sounds evoke creepy, spooky, fearsome effects. That's no coincidence. The connection between sound and fear is a strong one, and experienced horror writers use many sound-related techniques to scare their readers.

FOR SLIMY STUFF, SLIPSHOD WORK, UNDERHAND METHODS, LOWER CLASSES AND SLIPPERY SITUATIONS

The 'SL' can imply several different unpleasant, undesirable things. First, it suggests anything that's slimy to the touch or poses a risk of slipping: *slip, slide, slope, slime, slush, slug, slop, slither, sluice, slick, sludge*. It also hints at underhand methods and unethical behaviour: *slander, slur, slay, sleaze, sly,* or poor workmanship: *slapdash, slipshod, slacker*. Finally, it can be used to talk about people and places which are perceived as lower class, often with an implied negative slant: *slum, slang, slave, slut*.

To boost the effect, use additional words which don't have any of those meanings but carry the 'SL' sound: *slab, sling, slot, slow, sliver, slender, sleet, slalom, sleek, asleep, sloop, sleeve, slit, slice, slat, slogan, slash.*

As you can see, the 'SL' is almost always at the beginning of the word, and repeating it will create an alliteration. Take care not to repeat it often, or it will draw attention to itself instead of subtly influencing the reader's subconscious.

Usage examples: slivers of glass instead of glass shards, slinging a brick instead of throwing, slicing the bread instead of cutting.

When To Use 'SL' Sounds

- to hint at underhanded methods and unethical attitudes
- to suggest poor craftsmanship or dubious work ethics
- to show contempt for the lower classes
- when describing yucky things
- for Lovecraftian fiction with oozing slime
- when characters struggle to walk on a slope or slippery surface
- to suggest careless work and poor workmanship

Tip: consider mixing 'SL' with 'G' sounds to describe squalid living conditions, or contrasting it with 'H' to hint at a haughty character's arrogant attitude towards perceived inferiors.

'SN' FOR SECRET MOVEMENTS, CONTEMPT, TREACHERY AND SNEAK ATTACKS

The sound 'SN' in the English language evokes sneaking behaviour—slow, secretive, crawling movements: *snake, snoop, sneak*, devious attacks: *sniper, snare, snitch, snatch)*, and derogatory attitudes: *snide, snort, snub, snigger, snark*. Sometimes, the sound can also indicate sleep: *snooze, snore*.

Here are some other words you can use. Their meaning is neutral, but their sounds add to the paragraph's sneaky effect: *snivel, snooze, snuggle, snow, snip, snap, snack, snot, snail, snug, snore.*

By using several 'SN' words in a paragraph, you can emphasise the secretive, contemptuous underhanded manner of what's going on.

Usage example: the captive doesn't walk past the sleeping guard out into the rain—she sneaks past the snoozing guard out into the snow.

When To Use 'SN' Sounds

- quiet movements when the character cannot afford to be discovered
- featuring a devious, untrustworthy character
- showing a coward's behaviour
- one character disdains another
- spying, shadowing, stake-outs

'STR' FOR STRICT RULES, DISCIPLINE AND RESTRICTIONS

The 'STR' sound suggests that someone is in full control while someone else must obey or suffer punishment: *instruct, strict, strong, strain, strive, strenuous, stress, straight, straddle, astride, strop, constraint, struggle, strafe, strap, strangle, strike, stronghold.*

Other words with this sound effect: *stripe, strife, straw, stray, strategy, streak, stream, strumpet, strata, stretch, astral, straggler, strip, string, strut.*

A milder effect is possible when the sounds 'ST' and 'R' occur in the same word, but not together: *star, stern, stir, stark, store, story, stir, storm, stirrups.*

Usage examples: the dominatrix instructs her client how to kiss her boots, and she's strict about it. If he doesn't do exactly as told, her strong leather flogger will draw painful stripes on his buttocks.

When To Use 'STR' Sounds

- for scenes of punishment
- for merciless authority
- for relationships based on unequal power: student/teacher, child/parent, grunt/officer, apprentice/master, assistant/boss
- in erotic fiction for sub/Dom scenarios, discipline, bondage and restraint.

Tip: 'STR' and 'P' together create a sense of strict authority and merciless rule enforcement.

'TR' AND 'T+R' FOR TRICKERY, BREWING TROUBLE AND TERRIBLE WEATHER

When the 'T' and 'R' sounds combine in one word, they signal troubles, problems and plot complications: *torture, torment, tornado, terror, terrible.* The effect is intensified when the sounds are joined as 'TR': *betrayal, trap, trouble, treachery, traitor, trick, trial, atrocity, troll, tantrum.*

Other words you can use to add to the effect: *train, trek, trudge, tray, art, cart, wart, tart, heart, start, certain, tarantula, tar, rat, brat, prat, pert, pretty.*

Usage examples: the characters trek along the trail in search of the treasure, rather than hike along the path seeking a hoard. The meal may be flavoured with tarragon rather than rosemary.

When To Use 'TR' Sounds

- when showing the problems the characters face
- situations of betrayal
- when writing about a quarrel-seeking character who likes to stir up strife
- to subtly alert the reader's subconscious that there's trouble ahead, of which the characters are not yet aware.

'W' OVERWHELMING FORCES, WILD WEATHER AND ANYTHING WET

The untamed forces of nature are expressed powerfully by words with the 'W' sound, especially when relating to the weather and the wind: *windy, whirl, waft, billow, wilderness, weather.*

Even more strongly, 'W' represents anything to do with water: *wash, wave, water, wet, swamp, wade, swim.*

In addition to the weather- and water-related words, you can enrich those paragraphs with other 'W' sounds to increase the effect, for example: *sweat, sweet, wander, wonder, when, why, where, weak, wary, weary, weed, wobble, wood, witch, work, wool, waver, weight, window, war, warmth.*

Note that this effect applies even when the 'W' is not pronounced: *wreck, wring, wretched, wrath.*

Usage examples: the characters don't trudge through the marsh towards the birches, they wade through the swamp towards the willows. Instead of squeezing their damp garments, they wring the wet clothes. The breeze doesn't lash the forest, it whips through the wood.

When To Use 'W' Sounds:

- wild nature settings
- stormy weather
- sea voyages, especially heavy seas
- metaphorical storms, including overwhelming emotions
- unstoppable forces, such as invading hordes
- a powerful person's wrath

'Z' FOR DIZZINESS, CONFUSION AND TOO MUCH DRINK

The 'Z', although pronounced almost the same as 'S', has a different effect. It suggests that the character is disoriented or confused: *dizzy, haze, puzzle, fizzle, woozy, swizzled, sizzled, crazy, bamboozle, bizarre, sozzled, maze, dazed, puzzled.*

Other words with the same sound you can use to strengthen the effect: *zest, zoom, dazzle, sizzle, blizzard, wizard, nozzle, lazy.*

Usage examples: dazed, the character gropes her way through the maze of corridors. He wakes with a woozy head, puzzled about how he came to be in this place.

When To Use 'Z' Sounds

- when the Point-of-View character feels disoriented
- to create a dizzy, dazed feeling
- to suggest a drunken state of mind

Tip: is the character getting drunk at a celebration? Then combine 'Z' with 'CH' and 'J' or 'F'. Is an idler indulging in drink and drugs as a form of relaxation? Try 'Z' plus 'L'. If he drinks and drugs carelessly without thought of the consequences, use 'Z' and 'F'. For a punishing hangover, hit him with a combination of 'Z', 'D' and 'P'.

PART 2:
SOUND PLACEMENT AND RHYTHM

Now that you've chosen the right sounds, let's look at how to place them for best effect. We'll also explore other euphonic techniques such as sentence length and rhythm.

SPECIAL SPICE: ALLITERATION

When a sound is repeated at the beginning of two or more words close together, this is called 'alliteration'. It's the most effective way to place your sound, but if overdone it can sound silly, so use this technique with thought.

Here's an example of skilful use by bestselling author Janet Evanovich. Note how she alliterates the 'B', 'D' and 'G' sounds to enhance her description of this violent, depressing, grungy place:

*Fires were a common occurrence, leaving more and more buildings blackened and boarded, and discarded drug paraphernalia clogged garbage-filled gutters. (*From *Two for the Dough)*

Alliteration is an effective technique for creating impact. If you want to emphasise a sentence, perhaps for an emotional revelation or a shocking twist, or make the reader remember a certain phrase, try alliteration to make the section poignant and punchy.

The English language is perhaps the best language in the world for alliterations. The earliest literature in the English language used a lot of alliterations (e.g. *Beowulf*).

Alliteration is highly effective for audiobooks, performances and reading aloud. It also works superbly in humour, in poetry, for public speeches, for slogans, headlines and titles.

Next time you're stuck for a title for a story, play with alliterations. Examples: *Pride and Prejudice, Famous Five, Sense and Sensibility, The Pickwick Papers, Love's Labour's Lost, The War of the Worlds, Nicholas Nickleby, The Wind in the Willows, Of Mice and Men.*

In poetry, you can use a lot of alliterations, but in prose it's best to use them sparingly. I recommend no more than four words in a sentence, and not in every sentence. It often works well in setting descriptions, but not in dialogue.

Caution: strings of alliterations can be silly. This may be the effect you want if you write humour, but for most kinds of prose it's better to use alliterations sparingly.

How much alliteration you use is one of the aspects of your voice. You may like to use a lot, very little or none at all. Treat alliteration as a special spice: a pinch adds flavour, but too much spoils the meal.

DISCREET INSIDER JOBS: ASSONANCE AND CONSONANCE

When the in-your-face display of alliteration is too bold, try the barely-there effect of its cousins consonance and assonance.

Here, the repeated sounds are placed in the middle of words. Very few readers will notice the technique, even if you apply it a lot. It is subtle but it works.

Consonance: a consonant sound (such as 'S', 'P', 'B', 'SL') is repeated in the middle of several words close together.

Examples: *a ghostly presence, plucky attacker, jolly pleasures, washed by waves, apprehend the impostor.*

Assonance: a vowel sound (such as 'OO', 'OH', 'EE') is repeated in the middle of several words close together.

Examples: *nitty-gritty, as soon as she put on her boots, now the dog howled, fear squeezed her chest.*

To get a strong effect, you can combine assonance or consonance with alliterations of the same sound.

Example using 'S': *the housekeeper insisted it was a silly rumour, but I had heard the servants whisper about the secret of the ghostly presence.*

You can also place the assonance or consonance at the end of words, but be careful. If an assonance or a consonance-assonance combination is repeated at the end, this creates a rhyme: *blue/due, see/flee, haste/waste, dear/rear, squeal/deal, blue/due.* While rhymes are useful in poetry, in prose they tend to sound silly.

WHEN THE SOUND IS THE WORD: ONOMATOPOEIA

Sometimes, a word mimics a sound, or even is the sound. This is common in comic books, especially for loud noises: *Boom! Bang! Crash! Boing! Whoosh! Zap!*

This is called onomatopoeia. You can use it in prose fiction, but I advise against the raw form because it can look blatant and naive.

The English language allows a refined application: turn the sounds into a verb *(the door banged shut)* or a noun *(the door shut with a bang).*

Using this sophisticated variation creates subtle yet vivid effects. Any sound can be turned into a verb or noun, so let your creativity flow. When you want a fast-paced, exciting effect, choose the verb: *to boom, to bang, to boing, to whoosh, to zap, to clank, to shoosh.*

In addition, many English words are actually imitations of sounds, but have become so common that you may not think of them as onomatopoeia: *the tap drips, the chain rattles, the horse's hooves clip-clop, the cat meows, the horse whinnies.*

You can use onomatopoeia words in all kinds of vivid prose, but the biggest use is in writing for children. Young readers and listeners, whose vocabulary is still limited, can grasp onomatopoeic words. When you write about the clip-clopping hooves and the meowing cat, they can hear and visualise the scene.

When writing for other audiences, use blatant onomatopoeia sparingly, and apply refined versions mostly to descriptions you want to make vivid.

KEEP THE BEST FOR LAST: BACKLOADING

Here is a nifty technique to give your writing style more impact: structure paragraphs so the most powerful word comes at the end.

A paragraph break is a pause—and the last word before that pause lingers in the reader's mind. Make it count.

Often, restructuring the sentence is all it takes, or perhaps adding, deleting or replacing one word. Here are some examples:

Before
She knew she had to kill it.

After
She knew she had to kill.

Before
She had a painful headache.

After
Pain pounded in her skull.

Before
He felt the pain then.

After
Then he felt the pain.

Before
A child was in there.

After
In there was a child.

Short, evocative nouns, adjectives and verbs are best:

Here's a list for your inspiration: *death, dead, kiss, lust, betray, slay, blood, fear, die, kill, deep, cold, heat, dark, boil, pull, grave, grip, grasp, hope, sear, scream, thrill, scar, bone, flesh, skull, wound, pray, home, pain, soul, child, flee, trap, teeth, curse, escape, safe, love.*

These words, on the other hand, have no particular effect: *it, then, them, across, through, there, somehow, around, under, of, off, for, that, be, others, his, her.*

Words with just one syllable have more power than those with several, so you may want to use 'risk' rather than 'danger', and 'cat' rather than 'feline'.

Some writers try to backload every sentence, but this may be too much. Try to use this technique for the last word of most paragraphs, and definitely for the last word of each scene, because that's where the impact is greatest.

Try to use sound effects from the Sound Thesaurus for backloading some paragraphs. For example, your scene about a heroic deed could have paragraphs ending with 'foe' and 'blown', while paragraphs in a creepy scene might end in 'squeal' and 'scream'.

However, do this only if a word is a natural fit for the content. Don't weaken your content for the sake of sound.

A related technique is frontloading. The principle is the same—put the most evocative word at the beginning of the paragraph—but it doesn't need to be the very first word, just one of the first. The number of syllables doesn't matter either.

Frontloading serves to pull readers and listeners into the story, especially after a mental mini-break at the beginning of a new paragraph, scene or chapter.

<u>Before</u>
At regular intervals along the road, danger signs warned drivers.

<u>After</u>
Danger signs warned drivers at regular intervals along the road.

<u>Before</u>
With every step, the abyss loomed closer.

<u>After</u>
The abyss loomed closer with every step.

Even if you don't want to use this technique for every paragraph, try frontloading and backloading every scene's first and last sentence.

SENTENCE LENGTH: VARIETY AND PURPOSE

So far, we've listened to the melody of your writing. Now let's pay attention to the rhythm.

Rhythm in prose differs greatly from rhythm in poetry. Poets may use a basic da-doom-da-doom, or complex pattern with dactyl, trochee, anapest and other meters, but they always aim for rhythmic consistency.

As a prose writer, however, you need to create variety. As soon as the rhythm becomes predictable, the story grows boring and loses its hold on the reader.

The first and easiest consideration is sentence length. Mix long, medium and short.

Avoid sections where every sentence has almost the same length. The sentences in this paragraph are all ten words long. After the second sentence the lack of variety will show. From the fourth sentence on, the reader gets bored subconsciously. Then even a thrilling plot won't keep readers hooked. Don't risk losing your reader's attention because of this monotony.

Look at this instead. I'm now showing you a paragraph with similar content, but sentences of different lengths, which will create rhythmical variety. Readers won't be consciously aware, but the varied sentence lengths will keep their attention riveted. Try it. Mix short and long sentences, and the rhythm will enhance the story you tell.

Sentence length should also vary throughout the novel. Instead of creating an average of exactly 15 words (or 22 or 31) per sentence in every chapter, aim to use more punchy sentences in some scenes and more leisurely ones in other parts.

Adapt the sentence length so it reflects the pace of the moment.

Is this an exciting scene with fights, chases and rapid action? Use short sentences: *swords clanked. Martha raced across the road.*

This creates a sense of speed, urgency, breathlessness. Some sentences can be very short. Just fragments even. The faster the pace, the shorter the sentences. But don't overdo this. A scene with nothing but short sentences and fragments is dull to read. Insert some medium-length sentences too.

When the pace slows—because the characters are resting and in a contemplative mood—it's time to switch to the leisurely rhythm created by longer sentences: *all along the edge of the forest clearing, golden autumn leaves dance in the azure sky, like ageing ballerinas swirling in a final performance before settling to retire on the grassy meadow.* However, it's best not to use more than two long sentences in a row, or your writing may feel tedious to the reader. Insert a shorter sentence here and there.

Other factors can play a role in sentence length too: the target audience (children's books feature shorter sentences), the genre (the sentences in literary fiction tend to be longer), and your writing voice (William Faulkner uses longer sentences than Ernest Hemingway), but in this book we're looking purely at the effect of euphonics on the reader's or listener's psyche.

You can play with word length in the same way. Mix long, medium and short words to create a varied rhythm. In fast-paced action scenes, use a lot of short words (preferably with just one syllable) and in leisurely contemplative moments, apply many medium and some long words.

But be careful not to overdo this. Whole sections with nothing but short words sound mechanical, and clusters of multi-syllabic words can make your style pompous and clunky.

SENTENCE STRUCTURE

Another way to create a varied rhythm is to structure sentences differently. Keep some sentences simple, and embellish others with complex constructions.

Teaching syntax is beyond the scope of this guide, so I'll focus on just one strategy which is super-effective and easy to master even if you're grammar-clueless: simply vary how the sentences begin.

In the English language, the natural sentence structure is to start with the subject:

John...
Mary...
Mrs Smith...
Uncle Joe...
I...
He...
She...
It...
They...
My aunt...
The queen...
The warriors...
The dog...
The palace...
The moon...
A group...
Two riders...
Clouds...

This structure is solid. One or two sentences following this pattern are fine. Paragraphs where every sentence starts with the subject, however, have a monotonous rhythm. This paragraph here is an example. Three sentences in a row starting with the subject will make your writing dull. Some novice writers write a whole page in which every sentence starts this way. Readers soon grow bored.

Fortunately, it's easy to fix this. In this paragraph, I've varied the beginning of the sentences so each starts in a different way. This method creates a livelier rhythm and is more likely to hold the reader's interest. Although I don't want to set rules, I suggest you start no more than two sentences in a row with the subject.

So how do you vary the sentence start? Without delving into grammatical terms, here are some ideas to get you going.

Time

At once...
At dusk...
In the evening...
On Sunday
After...
At the same time...
When...

Place

Here...
Under the apple tree...
By the river...
At the gatehouse...
Close to the road...
Next to...
In her suitcase...
At the airport...
On the other side...
All across the nation...
Near the bottom of the page...
In a corner of the room...

Present Participle (that's the -ing form of the verb)

Dodging the bullet, she
Gasping for breath, he...
Racing down the stairs, she...
Trying to keep his mouth shut, he...
Humouring him, she....

Others

Although...
Despite...
However...
Against...
Luckily...
Nevertheless...
With...
Without...
Like a...
If...

There are many more, and it's worth applying your creative skills to finding the ones best suited to your story.

But don't rely on any one type, otherwise your writing becomes monotonous again. For example, if many sentences start with the Present Participle (often seen in novice writers' manuscripts), the story grows tedious to read.

REPEAT, REPEAT, REPEAT... BUT SPARINGLY, VERY SPARINGLY

To arouse the reader's emotions, repeat not just a sound, but a whole word. This technique needs to be applied with caution, because in the hands of an unskilled writer, it can fail.

Repeat three or more consecutive clauses containing the same word. These can be clauses in the same sentence linked by commas, or they can be separate sentences. The structure is not strict—sometimes the repetition is disrupted and restarts later.

Here are some examples:

Scrooge was his sole executor, his sole administrator, his sole assignment, his sole residuary legatee, his sole friend and sole mourner. (From *A Christmas Carol* by Charles Dickens)

It was the best of times, it was the worst of times, it was the age of wisdom, it was the age of foolishness, it was the epoch of belief, it was the epoch of incredulity, it was the season of Light, it was the season of Darkness, it was the spring of hope, it was the winter of despair. (From *A Tale of Two Cities* by Charles Dickens.)

I longed for the numb. I longed for the comatose state of the hospital. I longed for that IV bag and the free flow of anesthetics. (From *No Second Chance* by Harlan Coben—like many modern thriller authors, Coben uses this technique frequently)

She thrust herself out of her chair and paced about the floor, cursing Iris for bouncing her, cursing herself for her own insanity, and cursing Mr. Crew for not sending her the statement when she'd first written to him. (From *The Sculptress* by Minette Walters, another thriller author.)

Blessed are the poor in spirit, for theirs is the kingdom of heaven. Blessed are they that mourn, for they shall be comforted. Blessed are the meek, for they shall inherit the earth... (Jesus Christ, quoted by Matthew in the Bible)

As I watch the 109, I now know the meaning of the word 'fear', real stark staring fear, the sort of fear that few people possibly ever experience. (From *First Light* by Geoffrey Vellum)

How shall I speak of the house of war, in which Esarhaddon and I filled such exalted stations? In my time there I learned how to ride a horse and drive a chariot, how to fight with the sword, the dagger, the bow, and the javelin. I learned the forms of military courtesy. I learned tactics. I learned discipline and the leadership of men. And, most important of all, I learned arrogance. (From *The Assyrian* by Nicholas Guild)

With luck, Baryush would take the message to mean his enemy was free and waiting. With luck, he would rush into the tent alone. With luck, he would take a moment to see the naked captive tied to the table was Kirral, giving Dahoud time to strike. With luck, Baryush was an unskilled swordsman. With luck, a single quick slash to the throat would suffice.

Dahoud would need a lot of luck. (From *Storm Dancer* by Rayne Hall)

For those of you who like technical terms, the correct word is 'anaphora' if the word is at or near the beginning of the sentence, and 'epiphora' if it's at the end. Anaphora tends to fit better into prose fiction than epiphora.

You can use repetition several times in a novel, although I suggest not using it more than twice per scene. Some writers use it a lot, especially modern thriller authors.

When to use this technique:

- Moments of despair (consider layering with 'D' sounds)
- Moments of high tension
- Sections of telling rather than showing
- A leader rallying followers for a cause (consider layering with 'O' sounds)
- Dialogue in which a character presents an emotional appeal
- Rules and prohibitions (combine the technique with 'P' or 'N' sounds)
- Humour
- Internalisations - the character plans or assesses the situation

For internalisation, consider repeating the word 'if'. This is perfect when the PoV is plotting a hare-brained scheme, or is taking her chances against great odds, or if he realistically assesses how minuscule his chance of success is. This sentence conveys a lot of clear information to the reader without creating an info-dump, and it builds suspense. Furthermore, it addresses any implausibility issues by acknowledging them, and it makes the reader root for the protagonist. It can also serve to show that the PoV is unrealistic or delusional, or to add irony.

Examples:

If the guard took his lunch-break early, and if he left his keys on the table, and if she could reach far enough through the bars to grab them, then she would escape.

If Annabelle was still single, and if she came to the class reunion, and if she fancied short men with freckles, then she might consent to a date.

If only her husband stopped nagging, if he saw her perspective, if he admitted that she was right, then they could have a happy marriage.

If I memorise the complete works of Shakespeare, if I lose two stone before the audition, and if the casting agent appreciates my late great-grandmother's contribution to theatre, then he practically has to offer me the starring role.

Since an 'if and if and if' sentence draws attention to itself, use it sparingly—maybe once or twice in the novel.

HURRY OR TEDIUM? MAKE LISTS

Fiction writers often use lists—not bullet-pointed, in-your-face constructions but subtly woven into the narrative fabric.

In a Cosy Mystery, for instance, lists often hide an important clue:

Sherla Holm glanced at the bathroom shelves: hairbrush, shampoo, conditioner, curling tongs, nail varnish, aspirin... nothing out of the ordinary. Later, the reader will realise that the presence of curling tongs in the bathroom of a woman with natural curls reveals the identity of the murderer.

Lists can also serve to convey to the reader how the Point-of-View character feels, without spelling it out.

ASYNDETON FOR HURRY

Let's say the character is in a hurry. Instead of writing 'He did everything as fast as he could' or 'She was in a terrible rush', create a list—and leave out the word 'and'.

A list of items without any 'and' conveys that the character is alert, in a hurry, acting fast. It may even hint at panic, desperation, time running out.

Picture books, dolls, crayons, cuddly toys—she tossed everything into the trunk and slammed the lid.

She grabbed passport, toothbrush, underpants, and ran.

He searched the wardrobe, the laundry basket, the bathroom cabinet, the desk.

He rummaged through linen, frills, lace, silk—then his fingers hit steel.

She tried the front door, the back door, the window, the garage, the cellar hatch.

He dodged, blocked, sliced, slashed.

The technical term for this kind of list is 'asyndeton'. You can use it several times in the novel, especially in fast-paced scenes for fights, chases and escapes.

If you like, you can combine it with sounds from the Sound Effects Thesaurus—the 'R' sound works especially well.

An asyndeton implies that there are more items or objects than actually included in the list.

POLYSYNDETON FOR TEDIUM

When your Point-of-View character is bored with endless dull views and tedious tasks, you could simply write something like 'She was bored', 'He found the tasks tedious'—but those are telling and dull.

You may be tempted to show the tedium and let the reader experience it, by describing every dull detail. But then the reader will feel bored, and that's not how you want them to feel while they read your book!

The polysyndeton solves this problem by conveying the dullness or tedium in a single sentence. Simply create a list and insert the word 'and' or 'or' between all the items.

Examples:

The preacher droned on about how one must not bear false witness or covet the neighbour's lawnmower or fornicate or drink whiskey or cheat at cards.

The sunny weather lured, but she had to stay indoors and memorise trigonometry rules and French grammar and the dates of the English Civil War.

He tried to concentrate on the task while his wife jabbered about the price of petrol and the seating arrangements for the wedding and what the rector had said to the curate's sister and the correct way to shape onion dumplings.

Mary's stomach rumbled and she wanted to place her order, but John deliberated whether they should have the poached salmon or the winter vegetable stew or the garlic lasagne or the curried beef.

The polysyndeton can also be used to make a list of events memorable or to slow the pace or to convey inevitability or informality or exuberance.

You can use this sentence pattern several times in a novel, though I would not use it more than once or twice in a scene.

TEST YOUR EUPHONICS SKILLS

Now it's time to apply what you've learnt. Try for yourself how well you've mastered this aspect of the craft, and how it improves your writing.

Here are three mini assignments.

1. FAST PACE

In the story you're working on, identify a fast-paced section—perhaps a fight, race or chase scene.

Write or rewrite a short piece of it (I suggest around 100 words) where the action is especially quick. Use euphonic techniques to emphasise the fast pace.

I suggest the following: mostly short words, mostly short sentences, one asyndenton, several words with the 'R' sound, one or more other sounds as appropriate for the content.

Read it aloud, or better still, use a text-to-speech software to hear someone else read it. Does it sound faster-paced than your usual writing? Then you've won.

2. CREEPY LOCATION

Write a short section (around 100 words) describing a creepy place, if possible from a piece you're currently writing or revising. Mention noises—that's always a good trick for creating a creepy, exciting or scary atmosphere—and use several words with 'EE' and 'S' sounds.

Read it aloud, or listen to someone else reading it. Does it sound creepy? Great job!

3. PLEASURE OF LEISURE

Identify a moment in your current story when the Point-of-View character enjoys a restful, relaxing experience. This could be a break between arduous challenges, an erotic scene with slow, sensuous lovemaking, sunbathing on a sandy beach or a soak in a hot scented bath. Write around 100 words. Engage several senses—I suggest vision, hearing, touch (texture), smell, and perhaps taste and temperature.

Use euphonic techniques: a mix of medium and long sentences, some words of three or more syllables, and several words containing the 'L' sound. Depending on the content, you may want to add 'J/CH' or 'M' sounds as well.

Read the paragraph aloud or listen to it. Does it convey the sensuous, relaxed pleasure of the experience? Then you have mastered the skill.

SAMPLE STORY: TAKE ME TO ST. ROCH'S

Here's one of my ghost stories. As you read this, see if you can spot the euphonic effects I used, especially 'S' and 'EE' sounds and backloading.

Jean hated silence. It gnawed at her nerves and sapped her spirits, especially during night-time drives. Maybe she should give up teaching evening classes, and try to get by on her widow's pension alone. Or perhaps she should scrape together the money to buy a radio for her car.

In the darkness, the slopes of the Sussex Downs sank into valleys, and woodlands merged into fields. The windscreen wipers screeched across the glass, smearing dirt with the remnants of a November drizzle. At least the sound kept the silence out.

A hitchhiker pumped her arm up and down. Jean disapproved of hitchhikers on principle, but this might be an emergency. Why else would a girl hitch a night-time lift at a crossroads in the middle of nowhere?

Jean could do a good deed, and at the same time get stimulating conversation to kill this unnerving silence. She slowed the car. It stuttered to a halt, then the motor went dead. A battery replacement was long overdue.

Leaning across the passenger seat, she opened the door. "Do you need-"

The girl slid into the seat and crossed her arms over her chest "To Seelsden."

To Seelsden, PLEASE, Jean almost corrected. Young people these days had no manners. The girl had not even given her the chance to say that Seelsden was out of her way.

But to refuse would be rude, and besides, the girl might get picked up by a psychopath.

"Seelsden it shall be." The car hiccupped, but started on the fourth try.

"Do you live there?"

The girl shrugged.

"I'm Mrs Jean Mills. I teach in adult education. Local history, mostly. What about you?"

Another shrug. So much for conversation.

"Of course, these days it's not safe to reveal personal details to a stranger."

"I'm Anne."

After that conversational effort, the girl sank back into silence, with her arms tightly crossed and her chin on her chest

Jean glanced at her from the corner of her eye. She was about fifteen, skinny with an unhealthy pallor and the kind of dishevelled look favoured by teens. Her smell suggested that she had not had a bath for weeks and compensated with perfume. If so, the scent was badly chosen, over-sweet with an underlying note of something rotten. On the other hand, the odour might stem from a smoked substance. Jean thought it better not to ask.

The silence stretched for mile after mile. Silhouettes of trees and steeples stood black against a violet sky.

"That's Seelsden up there." Jean winked the indicator into action. "Where do you want me to drop you off?"

"St. Roch's."

St. Roch's, PLEASE, Jean wanted to correct, especially since that church was another three miles off her route. Once Seelsden's parish church, it now stood lonely and desolate on the ridge. Long ago, after an epidemic, the survivors had burnt their village and rebuilt it further away, leaving only the consecrated church in place.

But it was cold and dark, and the girl was tense. The way she kneaded her fingers in her lap, the way she hardly spoke a word. Heaven knew what bad stuff had already happened to her that night. Jean had a teacher's protective instincts. She would deliver the girl safely to her doorstep.

St. Roch's came into sight, a huge silhouette of silent stone. Not a single house in the vicinity.

"Where exactly do you live, Anne? I'll walk with you to make sure you're safe." Jean got out and clicked the car door shut. A damp chill wrapped around her.

"This is where I need to be." For the first time, the girl turned her white face towards Jean, and unclenched her arms. The stink spread. Something dark protruded from her chest: a piece of half-rotten wood.

"What the... do you... Are you hurt? I'll take you to hospital." Jean grabbed the handle of the driver's door.

Anne croaked a laugh. "It doesn't hurt, you know."

Jean berated herself for overreacting. This was nothing but a drug-induced prank. A belated Halloween party with fancy dress.

"But you must dig me a grave in there."

Jean adopted a stern tone. "The joke has gone quite far enough, Anne. I admit you've given me a fright with that phony stake, pretending to be a vampire -"

"Nah. Vampires aren't real, you know."

"Then what are you supposed to be? I mean, what archetype are you aiming to portray?"

"I'm a suicide, right?" Anne sounded proud, as if she had announced that she was a head girl or a carnival queen.

Jean recalled the custom of burying suicides at crossroads, with stakes through their hearts to stop them from rising. "Not many people will appreciate the difference, but as a historian, I congratulate you."

"Then you understand. I must get into the consecrated ground at St. Roch's." Anne pointed at the curving gate. "You'll bury me."

"Now listen. I agreed to drive you to Seelsden, and I gave you a lift here." Jean clung to her denial. "But I don't have the time to play games. Hop back into the car and I'll drive you home, wherever that is."

The girl pushed between Jean and the car, leaning insolently against the door. Jean grabbed her wrist to pull her out of the way. The flesh felt as squishy and cold as a wet sponge, with little substance.

Shock slammed into Jean's stomach. She stared, unable to move from the spot.

"Listen to me. I'll explain." Anne's wide eyes implored Jean. "Please."

The sudden courtesy did it. "Very well. I'll listen." The teeth of the car key cut into Jean's palm.

"I was murdered."

Jean grasped the contradiction as if it could cancel out the whole horrible unreality. "I thought you killed yourself?"

"My sweetheart's family wanted him to marry another. They wanted me dead." Anne's voice, though flat, vibrated with hatred. "They got their chance when my brother came back from Rome. He had the plague. They locked our whole family into the cottage, healthy and sick together. They shut their ears to our pleas, and waited for us all to die."

Jean sucked in a sharp breath. Putrid air passed through her throat. She was familiar with the tragedies of local history: crosses painted on the plague houses, doors nailed shut.

Euphonics for Writers

Suddenly words bubbled out of the girl's mouth. "I watched my mother die, my sisters. My brother and I survived. John never forgave himself for bringing this fate upon us." She kneaded her hands. "By the time I got out, my sweetheart was married. I killed myself."

Jean's hand holding the keys trembled. The fate of the plague victims had haunted her nightmares since she was a girl.

"I'm a good Christian. I need to rest in holy ground, and a human must do it. Please, Mistress Mills. The ground is soft. It'll only take half an hour."

Jean's knees were quaking, but she had to do this. Here was her chance to undo one of the horrors of history, to save one of the people she had pitied so much.

"Very well. I'll need to turn the car around to shine the lights." With shaking fingers, she fumbled the lock open, then the ignition. She manoeuvred until the headlights illumed the churchyard, but the car still faced down-slope so she could bump-start it later.

The car boot contained no toolbox, no shovel, not even a spoon. A rummage through the glove-compartment yielded a nail file.

The night was silent around the 13th century Norman stone church. Jean unlatched the heavy wooden gate. It creaked on its unoiled hinges. Jean's feet crunched gravel with every step. Anne moved without a noise.

In the blaze of the headlights the tree stems threw stripes across the ground, black on grey. Tombstones stood as pale pillars.

Anne pointed to her chosen spot.

Jean braced herself and ducked into the darkness of the deep-hanging branches. She hung her gabardine jacket over a crumbling tombstone, and placed her black pumps neatly next to it. Wind brushed her arms and neck, soft but cold. Kneeling, with her skirt tight around her legs, she stabbed the nail file at the earth to break it up. Fortunately weeks of persistent autumn rains had softened the local clay soil. When she pulled out the first tuft of grass, its roots teemed with silvery maggots.

Already, the twin lights from the car were dimming. Moisture seeped through her skirt and tights and chilled her knees. Her scalp itched. Despite the prevailing chill, sweat trickled from her armpits down her sides.

Her fingers groped their way in the cold slippery ground. The smell of fresh earth blended with the odour of dusty museums, of moor and decay. She touched something hard, sucked her breath in and examined the pale sliver. Probably a piece of bone from an earlier burial.

The light grew faint.

Above, something rustled in the silver-grey leaves. The twigs of the trees beckoned like skeleton fingers, withered and pale.

The church stood high and still, an indifferent observer.

"Would you mind talking?" Jean asked the girl. Even a ghost's voice was better than the void. "Tell me about what life was like in your day. Please."

"Dig faster."

Jean was already burrowing as fast as two bare hands and a nail-file allowed. She clawed and shovelled, shutting her mind to the question about how long it would take to dig a hole big enough to hold an adult body.

Then the light was gone and darkness descended.

The wind died away, and the silence became as suffocating as the darkness. There was no sound now but the thudding of earth on earth, and the occasional rustling of nettles against the fence.

As Jean's eyes adapted to the darkness, recognising its shades of grey, she could see the gravestones again. They stood erect in rows, large ones and small ones side by side like families in a procession.

Euphonics for Writers

"Don't look. Keep going," urged the girl.

Don't look at what? Jean strained to see. Was it the stones that were moving, or ghosts, approaching slowly, a bold noiseless army?

All further speculation was cut short. Something cracked, the sound of breaking stones, of a tomb bursting into pieces, and white silhouettes emerged everywhere.

"Dig, dig!" Ann stamped her foot on the ground. "You're nearly done. Don't let me down. They won't harm you, it's me they hate..."

"They?" Clutching her nail-file, Jean scanned the surroundings for an escape route. Ghosts were rising everywhere.

"My sweetheart's family," the girl stated flatly. "They begrudge me the Christian burial. They don't want me to lie next to their only son. Hurry up."

Already, a dozen pale spectres approached in slow silence.

Jean leaped out of the hollow to run.

The ghost clamped an icy hand around Jean's arm. "Don't stop now. You're nearly done. Once I'm buried, they've lost and will leave us alone."

Proving her point, she curled in the shallow hole. It would just take few more inches.

Jean dropped to her knees again to burrow in feverish fear. When she looked up, the spectres were looming above, wrapped in white tatters. Many had ugly swellings at the neck, and eczema covered their limbs like purple roses. Smells of cadaver and pus made Jean retch.

"They've... they've got the plague, haven't they?"

"It got them eventually," Anne said. "Hurry up."

A one-armed old man limped close, leaning over the grave. Purple nodes dotted his face, black blisters his swollen lips. A lifeless tongue hung out of his mouth, black and tainted with gore. Jean shrank deeper into the grave, where Anne was already cowering in the foetal position, her face buried in her arms.

From above, many inflamed, swollen eyes stared at her. Arms, full of open sores, reached out. Could they infect her with their touch? Had she been digging her own grave?

"Dig," the girl screamed. Her cold fist hammered Jean's legs. "They murdered me and my brother! Save me!"

Jean carved and tossed soil with bare fingers. She had to get the girl underground before the other ghosts reached her. Sweat drenched her blouse and blended with the dirt to dark smear.

Another inch down. And another.

Already several pairs of stinking arms reached out from above.

"Enough. Now cover me."

With both hands, Jean heaped earth on the slight form. Then she closed her eyes, and ran right through the cluster of ghosts, feeling their repulsive bodies touch hers, their fingers claw at her clothes. Breathless, she made it to the car.

She slid into the seat, slammed the door shut, shifted the gear to second, turned the key in the ignition. *Rrr-rtch. Rrr-rtch.*

On the third try, the motor jerked to life. She sped away from St. Roch's, away from Seelsden, back onto the main road she should never have left.

She was safe. Never in her life had she experienced such relief. With the heating turned on full, and with the familiar motor smell around her, warmth came back to her limbs, and the rapid heartbeat in her throat subsided.

What she needed was a big mug of hot tea with lots of sugar, and more importantly, a human voice to break the silence. A voice. Any voice would do. Preferably a young, chatty one. Preferably male. No more ghost girls.

A hitchhiker was pumping his arm by the roadside. She squealed the car to a stop.

"Thanks." The young man fell into the seat. "I'm glad you've stopped, Miss. Not much traffic on the road at this time of the night. I appreciate it. My name is John."

A polite passenger. Talkative. Just what she needed to return to reality. Even if he smelled awful. Why didn't young people bathe these days, and brush their teeth properly? But what did it matter, as long as he talked?"

"I'm Mrs Jean Mills. I teach adult education courses at the local college." Hearing her own voice was a relief. "I may not look respectable, but I am. My hands and clothes got dirty when I helped someone with an emergency." She kept talking, risking that this young man would think her a loony old bat. "I've had a horrid night. In fact, you probably won't believe me."

"I believe you, Mistress Mills." He shifted in his seat and cleared his throat. His odour intensified, sweet and foetid. "And I really appreciate what you did for my poor sister. Anne had waited so long. Now, will you take me to St. Roch's, please..."

Jean would have preferred silence.

SAMPLE STORY: THE COLOUR OF DISHONOUR

As you read this historical horror story, see if you spot the euphonic techniques I've applied. Note especially the liberal use of the 'P' sound, the alliterations, the backloaded sentences, the onomoatopoeia, and the way the sentence length shortens during the fast fighting action.

Caution: This story contains violence.

"Now!" At my command, the catapult timbers creak and sling a hundred balls of flaming pitch at the fortress.

I count the heartbeats until the response: sixteen, seventeen, eighteen. Amidst pillars of smoke, yells of fury shoot up.

This time, we've scored. My men howl in triumph.

"Again - now!" More fiery death rains into the defiant town.

They have no water left up there to put the fires out. After nine months of siege, the dogs of Ain Narnat will be forced to surrender at last.

If only they had yielded sooner, I would have preserved the fine houses, the carved ceilings, the graceful murals on their temple façades. Instead, they resisted, day after day, moon after moon, forcing me to drastic measures. I cut off their supplies, I drove them to thirst, and still the steep old walls sneered their defiance down at me.

I wait.

The desert heat bites. Sweat has glued the tunic to my back, mixed with the desert sand into a layer of cake that itches on the skin. I can't wait to get out of this accursed place, back to headquarters, back to civilisation.

Where's their envoy? How dare they make me wait!

The town smokes, the screams do not abate, but still the gate doesn't open.

I march up and down the line of my men, shoulders squared, chin raised, bold confidence in every step. A general never falters, never admits even a seed of doubt. And I'm a good leader, one of the greatest. Have I, War Tribune Karamak, not brought down hordes of rebels and tribesmen, and conquered more than two score fortresses for the Queendom?

They defy me still? A curse upon their ancestors!

I've led enough sieges to know the state of despair behind their barred doors, with their cisterns long depleted, their food supplies cut off long ago. They're drinking their own piss, grateful for every sip of it. They're sucking the bones of rats and devouring the flesh of their dear dead.

Those fools should have yielded the moment my legions marched towards them. I offered generous terms then. They would have been permitted to live on much as before. What difference would it have made to them if the banner flying from the tower was the Zigazian Goat or the Quislak Bull?

As a siege draws out, terms always get harsher. Threats of slavery, rape and slaughter usually lead to early surrender on easy terms. But the people in this accursed town thought they could hold out against the might of Quislak's legions.

I tightened the terms moon after moon, gave them many chances to cave in before it got worse. They've paid for their obstinacy with hunger and fear, and it has gained them nothing. Now we've reached the stage where few mercies are offered. Surrender is no longer an easy option. Some will kill themselves rather than fall into our hands alive.

Fine. It saves us the tedious chore of torture and execution.

Still the gates remain shut. There's no point waiting in this accursed heat. I'll launch another attack under cover of darkness tonight to finish them off.

"Collect enemy arrows!" I order my men. Nothing valuable is to be wasted. "Gather the wounded and the dead."

Soldiers scurry about like ants swarming from a heap. Our own losses are small.

"Stand down. Withdraw behind ramparts! Honour and glory!"

"Honour and glory!" the soldiers shout back. They, too, are long tired of this campaign, impatient to loot and rape and then get back to their wives.

While the officers march the soldiers back to their tents, I stare up at the citadel.

The town's towers and turrets gleam golden in the afternoon sun, pretending peace. The yellow curtain wall still rises from bare rocks the way it has for centuries. After repeated batterings from catapulted rocks, it still admits no more damage than a couple of cracks.

"Sir!" One of my officers, Tarik marches towards me with rapid strides. A promising young man. I'll see to his promotion when I get mine.

"What is it?"

"With your permission, Sir. Word has arrived that Ain Zabarzin has fallen."

"Djinns of Darkness!" My stomach churns.

"It is good news, is it not, sir?"

Good news? For the Queendom of Quislak, indeed. Not for me. Mother of Mares, am I supposed to rejoice at my rival's success? That's the third town that upstart Dahoud has conquered while I waited outside this accursed citadel like a hungry cat before a mouse hole.

"Very good news," I say, though the words taste sour in my mouth. "Give the men an extra ration of wine."

Euphonics for Writers

My chances for promotion evaporate faster than a trickle of rainwater on desert sand. There's one opening for the rank of General, and it ought to be mine. I can't have Dahoud beat me to it, that uneducated upstart, just because of those dogs in the yellow town up there. If they want to starve, let them, but I won't let them ruin my career.

I wish I could rip those defiant walls apart with my bare hands. I'd like to grab and throttle every neck in there, and punch their faces and tear out their entrails.

Until dusk, I deal with administrative matters, requesting provisions and preparing the night's attack.

Just before darkness falls, another herald gallops into my camp. The message is for my personal attention. I rip it open.

The High General Paniour greets War Tribune Karamak: The Tribune Dahoud will take over the siege of Ain Narnat. Ensure everything is in order and prepared for the command handover when he arrives on the third day of the new moon.

Djinns of Darkness! How dare he treat me like this, after decades of sacrifices and successes in the service of the Queendom! Boiling with fury, I grind my teeth and clench my jaw so tight, it hurts.

I'll show them. I'll subdue this town before Tribune Dahoud arrives, and make its people pay for this humiliation.

As I stride towards the command tent, a calm settles over me, dangerous and deadly.

I allow my gaze to travel over the trophies and treasures from previous wars, captured standards, looted silverware and masterfully crafted works of art. My smile caresses the bronze statues, shaped by long-dead artisans. These souvenirs of my glorious career confirm that the current campaign, too, must be won.

And suddenly I know how.

I call Lieutenant Tarik and, in a low voice, dictate a letter, outlining a change in surrender conditions. Up to now I've acted in accordance with custom, the harshness of the surrender conditions increasing every moon. We might let some of the women live, use them and sell the healthy ones. For the men, they won't dare to hope for even a quick death. They'll be stunned with joy when I offer to revert to the terms of nine moons ago, to let them live their lives and keep their possessions in return for opening their gates.

Tarik's eyes narrow, and his brows pull together. "These terms are unusually generous, Sir."

"So they are." I snatch the parchment and fold it, sharpening the folds with my thumbnail. I drip a dollop of pale wax on the edge and press my dagger hilt into it, imprinting my personal seal.

"But, Sir. No disrespect, Sir, but if we lessen the severity, won't it set a bad example?"

I know what he means. If word spreads that these people were allowed to go free, other towns won't take our harsh terms seriously. They'll all hold out for better conditions. But I don't care about other sieges in other places. I want this town, and I want it today.

"Just take the envoy staff and deliver the message," I snarl.

"Yes, Sir." The lieutenant salutes.

*

When the sun sends the first shy rays across the plain, I receive the enemy envoy in my command tent.

He looks as weak as if he could barely carry the spiral staff. His arms are thin stalks and his eyes haunted hollows, and he smells like something a dog has dragged out of a latrine ditch.

I offer him a cushioned seat, and smile like a gracious host. I pour citron water with floating sprigs of honeybalm for him, Lieutenant Tarik, and myself.

When food arrives - succulent golden dates, flat bread and fresh pink-skinned figs, my guest's struggle between greedy hunger and refined reticence amuses me.

"Eat, good man," I say with an expansive gesture of my hand.

Not waiting to be asked twice, the man gobbles and gulps. "Sir, Tribune Karamak, how can we thank you for your mercy? The entire town prays to the Mighty Ones to reward your mercy. We accept your generous terms with great humility." He pauses. "If you truly mean them."

"You have my word." I speak in clipped tones, as if insulted. I point to the bull standard that towers above the table. "Honour and Glory, the motto of the Quislak legion. None of our officers has ever broken his word." I wave away the flies that try to settle on the glazed dates.

The man casts his eyes down. "Please accept my apologies. I did not mean to doubt your words, only to clarify their meanings." He hesitates. "Will the women be harmed?"

I choke back laughter at his delicate phrasing. The right to rape is part of a siege soldier's pay.

"The men will not touch them."

The promise makes Tarik look up so sharply he spills citron water from his beaker.

"You may return now, and prepare for the surrender. Your leaders will open the gates and give the town into my rule."

The envoy salutes, picks up his staff, and strides off with more energy in his step than when he had arrived.

I summon my senior officers. "Tomorrow, the town will be ours." I point at the thin figure hurrying up the steep track, the staff clutched in his arms. "That man turned traitor to his people. He will open the gates for us."

They nod sagely. Experienced warriors, they know that treachery is common in times of war, and often brings sieges to an end.

Tarik's mouth opens. His eyes widen, his brows rise. "But Sir, he didn't…"

"Return to your duties, Lieutenant!"

I'll keep an eye on him for the rest of the day.

*

My heart beats like a kettledrum. It always does before a big offensive. I survey my soldiers as they stand in silent formation before the gatehouse, their hands on the scimitar hilts.

Since the defenders expect us to march into their town, they'll see nothing suspicious about this. I even signal my drummers and trumpeters to rouse a musical salute.

The heavy wooden door of the inner wall creaks open, followed by the copper-clad outer gate.

I lead my troops, with Lieutenant Tarik at my shoulder. At a flick of my hand, the soldiers leap. They slash, hack, batter and slash. Blades flash, blood spurts. Dead bodies drop.

Trumpets and cymbals drown out the screams.

"Sir!" Tarik protests. "You gave your word-"

My own blade cuts him off, silencing the only witness of my promise. In the general carnage, no one notices, or if they do, they're too wise to speak up.

Townspeople scurry into hiding holes, tumbling down into cellars to escape the carnage. Covered under clutter, they cower in corners.

"Find the cowards! Drag them into the daylight and kill them!" I wave my red-dripping weapon. "Use the women as you will!"

"Yes, Sir!" My men raise their swords. Having waited nine moons for this moment, they share my pent-up rage. I know their mood. It's always the same after a siege. Angry men throw themselves into rampage, rape and slaughter.

Later, regrets will come for the tender-hearted ones among them. After my early sieges, I felt bad for the victims. But I have no sympathies for these bastards who so nearly cost me my career.

Bleeding bodies get tossed aside, piled up like soup meat ready for the cauldron.

I point to the temple forum. "Put the corpses into orderly heaps over there for now. Erect structures to hang them from. Let them dangle by their feet. All of them – the living, the dead. Then I want to see their blood. Slice off their heads and hands so the blood runs. Gather it in vessels – tubs, amphoras, jugs, whatever you find. And then," I bellow in my loudest voice, "Paint this town red! Let the walls drip with the bastards' blood!"

Already the soldiers bring brushes and brooms, and dip them into the buckets of blood. One building after another gets splashed crimson. Swarms of flies flock to them, black blotches on red.

"With due respect, Sir…" The troop healer keeps hands clenched before him and his head bowed. "From a hygiene standpoint, this measure is not advisable. Blood attracts disease."

I wave away his concerns. "In this climate, the liquid will dry quickly. I'll tell the men to wash when they've finished."

I march on to inspect what artwork has been salvaged: a few bronze statues, some pottery.

"Where's Lieutenant Tarik?" I bellow. "I want him to draw up the inventory."

The statue-sorting soldiers stare at me, wide eyed.

"Sir." The speaker doesn't raise his eyes from the figure in his hands. "Lieutenant Tarik is dead. He…."

Another says quickly: "He fell during the taking of this town."

Then they both pull away, duck their heads, and bury themselves behind the statues.

I grunt and leave them to their duty. I have work to do.

*

Installed in the governor's tower, where the north windows command superb views of dangling bodies, I dip my quill in ink.

The War Tribune Karamak greets the High General Paniour. I have conquered Ain Narnat, adding to the glory and honour of the Queendom of Quislak. Of course, the Tribune Dahoud is welcome to inspect the scene of this success.

A small splotch of red appears on my palm, as if I'd just squashed a sated mosquito. I ignore it.

*

Two days on, soldiers complain of itching sores and burning stomachs. After four days, a score are dead.

The High General's letter of congratulations allows me to blot out those concerns, but not for long.

"I warned you, Sir," the troop's healer said. "All the blood on the walls brought squirrelflies and silvergnats, and they carry disease."

"Nonsense," I snap. "Nothing to do with the blood. It's the water, as usual. The Narnatians threw corpses into the well, an old trick to murder the conquerors. I've seen it often enough."

"With due respect, Sir. The town had cisterns, and those are empty. As for the wells on the slope, you ordered them bricked up. Our water comes from a brook in the mountains."

"Get out!"

When twenty-six die the following day, and forty-one the day after, I amend the records. Deaths remain deaths, of course, and cannot be denied. I've lost more men in this town than Dahoud in three campaigns. But at least I can ensure they succumbed to war wounds. The documentation looks better this way – more honourable.

It seems I've cut my finger somehow. A string of crimson beads appears, though when I wipe it, the skin seems unblemished. Strange.

*

Another missive. The High General Paniour wishes to inspect the town. Worry gnaws at my guts. If truth about the surrender comes out – if anyone discovered the blood on my hands - I'll be court martialled for both breach of promise, and for offence against Quislak honour. This would be the end of my career. They'd strip me of my rank and glory, and send me to spend the rest of my life dragging stones in the quarries.

Fortunately, no one lives who has witnessed enough to tell the tale.

Still, I order the citadel whitewashed, the corpses consigned to the flames, destroying all reminders of the violent conquest.

*

Today we receive the High General. The town gleams in peaceful white, its innocence restored. Only a faint smell of sweet-roasted flesh lingers.

"Honour and Glory, Sir!" I salute.

Something sticks in my palm, like the prick of a needle, and a drop of red grows. What is this? Quickly, I wipe my hand on my sleeve.

In the newly erected shrine of the Mighty Ones, lined with looted statues, I sprinkle granules of frankincense on the braziers. Again, my palm stings. I open my hand, watch the red beads form as if I was holding a necklace. I close my fist, flick it back open. I see a red smear, nothing else. No visible wound. Weird. There must have been something in the incense that snagged my skin.

I stick with the ritual, but with every prayer, every vow, my pulse brings up a little more blood. It starts to seep between my fingers.

With pride, I carry the sacred banner of Honour and Glory for the soldiers' parade. The bronze-embroidered bull sparkles in the sun.

My palms sweat, and the pole starts to slip in my perspiring hands. Then I see a thin stream of blood slither down the pale wood.

Luckily, no one notices, and I swallow my scream.

*

As soon as I can disengage myself, I rinse my hands thoroughly and inspect them for signs of injury. Nothing.

I visit the healer, who says he sees not even a scratch.

"But I've been bleeding all morning," I insist. "Sometimes there's blood, sometimes there isn't. It comes and goes. Do something about it."

"Sir, you've been under a lot of pressure recently…"

"Are you suggesting I'm making this up?"

"Far from it, Sir." The healer's face remains free of expression. "I'll give you a healing cream."

I snatch the proffered jar and leave.

*

During the meal, of roast lizard in honey and pepper sauce with fine Darrian wine, the High General displays the finest table manners and elegance of movement.

I, on the other hand, appear clumsy like a peasant, because my palms are bleeding softly, and I'm forced to keep at least one of them curled up most of the time, clutched around an absorbent pad. I can't even pour the wine for fear of dripping blood into his beaker. I hope the fine workmanship of the Narnatian beakers – the finest of the loot – will keep my guest's attention. We talk a lot of warfare, of honour and glory. When we rise from the table, I barely manage to conceal the stains on my tunic.

*

I order tubs of hot water brought, add plenty of ground-up soapberries, and toss my clothes in for an overnight soak.

Before going to bed, I rub the healing cream thickly all over my hands, but when I wake in the morning, I find my sheets smeared with blood.

My palms bleed more frequently today. Every hour I have to cleanse them, and I carry a supply of linen scraps and moss with me.

How am I going to go through tomorrow's town inspection, without showing I have blood on my hands? I put on my old wine-coloured tunic, which won't show the stains so much, although it is a little frayed at the sleeves. Despite the glowing heat, I wrap myself in my heavy woollen cloak which allows me to hide my hands in its flowing folds.

Conducting the dignified High General through the conquered town, past the white-washed and plastered walls, I point out the cracks inflicted by his catapults, the scorched ruins that proved his firebolt's efficiency.

I talk at length about the murals of the temple façades which, although damaged by smoke and fire, still hold on to some of their former glory. Perhaps the Queendom's own artists can restore them. My talk demonstrates artistic sensitivity and distinguishes me from other, uneducated conquerors.

I wished I could use expansive gestures to stress what I'm saying, but I feel the seeping between my fingers and keep my fists discreetly curled around absorbent pads of moss. My movements come across as cramped and clumsy, not at all like those of a successful War Tribune.

Does the High General see something amiss? He seems to study me strangely. His glances flick between the walls and me. Is he suspecting what lies beneath the gleaming white?

To distract him, I speak quickly. "I had the walls cleansed and painted, a measure of hygiene. You will, I'm sure, agree with me on the importance of hygiene. It's something younger tribunes still have to learn, especially when they don't have the benefits of a good education."

He seems to digest this snide hint at Dahoud's inferior style, but keeps silent.

Despite my firmly clenched fists, blood seeps again. I feel it welling up wet between my fingers.

I talk faster, louder. "I acted honourably, I truly did. All in accordance with the old customs. I offered them good terms. It was their own fault that they refused. The conquest was honourable." I keep my hands hidden, wrapped in the folds of the woollen cloak. No doubt by now the moist stains start to show, but I dare not look down. Sweat pours from my brow, from my armpits, runs down my sides. Blood wells like water from two eager springs. My breath shortens, becomes a pant. "Honourable, Sir. I vow." Blood mingles with sweat, both pour freely. Already their streams slither down my thighs.

"Honour. All in good honour," I insist.

Down my calves. *Drop. Drop.* On my feet.

On the stones. *Dropdrop. Dropdropdrop.* I dare not look down. How much longer can I distract him?

"The gatehouse," I pant. "Let's go there. I want to show you something." I don't know what, but we have to move, before he discovers the blood pooling around my feet.

The cloak's hem sloshes wet around my ankles. I gather it up, clutch it as best I can. Oh, let them leave, let them leave! Behind me, soldiers whisper. They will have seen.

Still, I keep on. "I hosted their envoy. Gave him everything. Figs. Dates. Glazed ones…"

As we walk downhill, the blood runs faster than my feet can stride. My sandals slip on the wet stones.

The hole in my hands is big now. Enough blood has escaped to fill a flagon. No, to fill buckets. And still Paniour does not speak. He does not even look at my hands. He only studies my face, as if seeking confession in my eyes.

But my witnesses are dead, they cannot intrude. If only the blood would stop.

Then it hits me. Of course, that's it. He wonders why I'm walking with bleeding hands. I'll stop the pretence.

I disentangle my arms from the cloak, hold them out, a dark-soaked pad of moss on each palm. "I injured my hands. Just a small injury. Take my hands, Sir, examine them, study them."

He frowns. "What do you mean?"

Blood pours like wine from two barrel spouts. It splashes Paniour's smart uniform.

I apologise. "I'm sorry, Sir, this blood, the blood on my hands..."

He looks grim now. His hand is on his dagger hilt.

I drop on my knees. "I didn't mean to dirty your tunic, Sir. Forgive me!" I beseech him, stretching my hands towards him. Rivers of crimson run along my arms, waterfalls cascade right down on the stones. Enough spurts to fill buckets.

"Are you sick?"

"It's the blood, Sir, don't you see? The blood on my hands!"

His eyes narrow, his lips thin. The whispers around me draw closer.

Seeing my life force drain away from me, I weep. Already the loss weakens me. My head spins. A feeling of dizzy emptiness spreads. How can a single body contain so much blood?

On my knees, I plead the soldiers to gather the blood, not to let it waste in the gutters, to collect it in vessels. I'm sitting in a pool of it, my garments soaked crimson. Flies flock to me, forming dark buzzing clouds.

Nobody moves.

"This man is sick," the High General says. "He's not fit to lead a legion and keep a citadel. The Mighty Ones be thanked, the Tribune Dahoud is already on his way to sort this place out."

Blood keeps running, swells like a river, splashes against the brilliant white walls, painting the town red.

DEAR READER,

I hope you enjoyed this book and have gained many practical ideas how to refine prose.

I'd love it if you could post a review on Amazon or some other book site where you have an account and posting privileges. Maybe you can mention what kind of fiction you write, and which of the techniques suggested in this guide work best for your stories.

Email me the link to your review, and I'll send you a free review copy (ebook) of one of my other Writer's Craft books. Let me know which one you would like: *Writing Fight Scenes, Writing Scary Scenes, The Word-Loss Diet, Writing About Magic, Writing About Villains, Writing Dark Stories, Writing Short Stories to Promote Your Novels, Twitter for Writers, Why Does My Book Not Sell? 20 Simple Fixes, Writing Vivid Settings, How To Train Your Cat To Promote Your Book, Writing Deep Point of View, Getting Book Reviews.*

My email is raynehall00000@gmail.com. Also drop me a line if you've spotted any typos which have escaped the proofreader's eagle eyes, or want to give me private feedback or have questions.

You can also contact me on Twitter: https://twitter.com/RayneHall. Tweet me that you've read this book, and I'll probably follow you back.

If you find this book helpful, it would be great if you could spread the word about it. Maybe you know other writers who would benefit.

At the end of this book, you'll find an excerpt from another Writer's Craft Guide, *Writing Vivid Settings*. I hope you enjoy it.

With best wishes for your writing and successful author readings. Wow the audiences with your work!

Rayne Hall

ACKNOWLEDGEMENTS

Sincere thanks to writers who critiqued the chapters: Larisa Walk, Douglas Kolacki, Judith Walker, Jess Mahler, Phillip T. Stephens, and members of the Professional Authors group, and also to the beta-readers who checked the entire manuscript before publication: Melissa Tacket, Johannes Matlaisane, Victoria Lynn Osborne, Joshua Walcher and Charles Matthews.

The cover design for this book and others in the Writer's Craft series is by Erica Syverson. The cartoon illustrations are by Hanna-Riikka. The proofreader is Julia Gibbs.

SAMPLE: *WRITING VIVID SETTINGS* *(Writer's Craft Book* **10**)

CHAPTER 1: SMELLS FOR REALISM

Here's a powerful technique for immersing readers into your story: use the sense of smell.

Of all the senses, smell has the strongest psychological effect. The mere mention of a smell evokes memories and triggers associations in the reader's subconscious.

Mention a smell, and the scene comes to life. Mention two or three, and the reader is pulled into the scene as if it were real.

A single sentence about smells can reveal more about a place than several paragraphs of visual descriptions. This is useful if you aim to keep your descriptions short.

For example, the hero enters a home for old people. *The place smelled of boiled cabbage, urine and disinfectant.* These nine words are enough to convey what kind of old people's home this is, and it creates a strong image in the reader's mind.

Or try these:

The room smelled of pizza, beer and unwashed socks.
The room smelled of beeswax, joss sticks and patchouli.
The corridor smelled of mould and leaking sewage.
The kitchen smelled of coffee, cinnamon and freshly baked bread.
The kitchen smelled of burnt milk, overripe pears and bleach.
The garden smelled of lilacs and freshly mown grass.
The cell smelled of blood, urine and rotting straw.

HOW AND WHERE TO USE THIS TECHNIQUE

The best place to insert a sentence about smells is immediately after the Point-of-View (PoV) character has arrived at a new location. That's when humans are most aware of smells, so it feels right if you mention them.

Smells trigger emotions. If you want your reader to feel positive about the place, use pleasant scents. To make the reader recoil, mention nasty odours.

Also, consider the genre. Thriller and horror readers appreciate being taken to places where odours are as foul as the villain's deeds, but romance readers want a pleasant experience, so treat them to lovely scents.

If you like, you can use this technique in almost every scene. To keep it fresh, vary the sentence structure and the wording. Here are some suggestions:

The place reeked/stank of XX and YY.
The odours of XX and YY mingled with the smells of CCC and DDD.
Her nostrils detected a whiff of XX beneath the smells of YY andCCC.
The smell of XX warred with the stronger odour of YY.
The air was rich with the scents of XX and YY.
The smell of XX failed to mask the stench of YY.
The stench of XX hit him first, followed by the odour of YY.
Beneath the scent of XX lay the more ominous odours of YY and CCC.
The scents of XX and YY greeted her.
The smells of XX and YY made his mouth water.
He braced himself against the stink of XX and YY.

PROFESSIONAL EXAMPLES

These examples show how authors have used this technique in their fiction.

The room smelled like stale smoke and Italian salad dressing. (Michael Connelly: *The Poet*)

I took a couple of deep breaths, smelled rain, diesel and the pungent dead-fish-and-salt stench off the river. (Devon Monk: *Magic to the Bone*)

The place smelt of damp and decay. (Jonathan Stroud: *The Amulet of Samarkand*)

A rare south wind had brought the smell of Tyre to last night's landfall: cinnamon and pepper in the cedar-laced pine smoke, sharp young wine and close-packed sweating humanity, smoldering hemp and horse piss. (Mathew Woodring Stover: *Iron Dawn*)

The smell hit her first: rotting flesh, ancient blood. (Kristine Kathryn Rusch: *Sins of the Blood*)

The air held the warm odours of honey and earth, of pine resin and goat sweat, mingled with the scents of frying oil and spice. (Rayne Hall: *Storm Dancer*)

Its air was stagnant, smelling of corner must, discarded tires, and jugs of used motor oil. (Janet Evanovich: *One for the Money*)

*The cold air reeked of cabbages and sweat. (*Jason Goodwin: *The Snakestone*)

The air simmered with the reek of garlic and hair pomade (Lindsay Davis: *The Silver Pigs*)

MISTAKES TO AVOID

If the first sentence in every scene is a list of three smells, it becomes predictable and boring. Make it less obvious by varying the wording, the sentence structure and the placement.

Don't overdo the bad smells, or the reader may feel such revulsion that she doesn't want to read on.

ASSIGNMENTS

1. Whatever story you're working on right now, whatever scene you're writing, think of two or more smells that characterise the place. Write a sentence about them, and insert it near the beginning of the scene.

2. When you go somewhere today—to the supermarket, the dentist or the church—pay attention to the smells of the place. Write them down. If you do this for a different place every day, you'll soon have a reference—a Setting Descriptions Bank—you can draw on for future stories.

Printed in Great Britain
by Amazon